AnD Sᵒ WAX Was MAde & Alsᵒ HONeY

AMy bᵉᵉder

T|P

Library of Congress LCCN: 2020942364
ISBN-13: 978-1-946482-36-5

Cover art: Manuel Philès (1275-1345), *Bestiaire*, Folio 18. Bibliothèque Sainte-Geneviève, Paris. Used by permission.

Cover design by Kenji Liu
Text design by Erica Mena and Kenji Liu

First paperback edition December 2020

Tupelo Press
P.O. Box 1767
North Adams, Massachusetts 01247
(413) 664-9611 / Fax: (413) 664-9711
editor@tupelopress.org / www.tupelopress.org

Tupelo Press is an award-winning independent literary press that publishes fine fiction, non-fiction, and poetry in books that are a joy to hold as well as read. Tupelo Press is a registered 501(c)(3) non-profit organization, and we rely on public support to carry out our mission of publishing extraordinary work that may be outside the realm of the large commercial publishers. Financial donations are welcome and are tax deductible.

ACKNOWLEDGMENTS

Many thanks to the editors of the following journals where these poems appeared:

AGNI: "Among Us," "Prodigious Fine Land," "Ovid on the Poor Economy of Overgrazing"

American Journal of Poetry: "After the Last Return," "And So Wax Was Made & Also Honey Out of the Tears of Re," "From A Practical Guide to Hand Analysis [last seen]"

Cerise Press: "Ancient Roman Poems Reveal Malaria" "In Central Asia Nomadic Horsemen"

Connotations Press: "Whole Cities Burn for Your Account Number," "Though from a Distance it Looked Like a Prison," "The Society for the Prevention of Premature Burial Thanks You"

december magazine: "Three Meals" "Nonce for the Gizzard"

Denver Quarterly: "From A Practical Guide to Hand Analysis [urchin]" "From A Practical Guide to Hand Analysis [ravine]"

Gettysburg Review: "Assume the Milk-White" "Physician, Priest or Gravedigger"

The Kenyon Review: "Letter from Inmate 0709-609" " The House of Être"

Michigan Quarterly Review: "Leviathan"

Plume: "Hatfield," Isle of The Narrator," "Ouija Blink" "The Madness of Crowds"

Poetry: "Dear Drought," "Lithium Dreams" "For Fresno's Best Process Server call Hermes," "A French Piano Tuner & a One-Eyed Glassblower Walk Into a Bar" "The Jealous Minor Gods," "Sir Say Pray," "With a Court of Flies Attendant"

Poetry Daily: "Assume the Milk-White"

32 Poems: "My Family Versus Yours"

CONTENTS

Light broke the needles, but cold took the blame—

The Jealous Minor Gods

I have hidden your lost teeth in the net of all my famous hair
And with foresight promised your umbilicus

To several minor gods. I paid your fee in fawn-skin
& the lightest fringe of tissue, all the quiet noons assembled,

In yard stars & the light of phosphorescent pens,
The dioramas that it takes to fill lacunae, in ancestral knots

That tell the story of our humble people: watchmakers,
Mainly, ventriloquists & scholars of quintessence,

Amateur lifeguards I meant to surpass. How I loved
My green & distant futures! But I love you more

From late Holoceme out to the farthest buoy, unto
Blackmail & a verb that means renouncing Christ

Or else describes the path of sap before it's amber,
Before it dimples, just a little, to collect—

from A Practical Guide to Hand Analysis *[last seen]*

if the islands of mystery are found between the lines of destiny
& life, I'm pretty sure we'll never know your fate
even if we do find some clue or explicable cause
in your overcoat pocket: a stag tooth or five Belgian francs,
a totem, a ticket with venue erased. Better,
a Kodachrome slide of rogue borealis. Or better,
a feather. The manor you lorded is charging admission;
they've erected a stone! How like you to vanish
last seen in a headline beekeeping, or boarding a Cessna
apace with your bronze-age valet. Meanwhile
the rest of us pause here. Abandoned, we gamble,
quarrel abjectly & drink. You could be in Rome.
If you're not inhabiting piazza pigeons please write.
If you're stuck in a crevice in Malapais, whistle—

Ancient Roman Bones Reveal Malaria: A Love Song

How like a hive, his body—so busy with rigor,
with languor & sweats: his spleen my arena,
his spine my near *vicus*, encampment. Ague
as opiate: I have bequeathed him these visions
of wings, my crepuscule sulks, a fever & tremor,
a ribcage too meager to scaffold a temple

or cistern of piss. Citizens, I'll never leave him—
not while forests are cleared by your hunger
for villas, for mainmasts, flagpoles & bonfires.
We'll wax as we dwindle, gut-swollen and rank.
What will be left for the Gauls? A cattail garden.
Shards & a damp palm's mark on the parchment.

Letter from Inmate 0709-609

He wrote I recently read your poem in a Review &
wonder would you be willing to engage in occasional

correspondence regarding for example how vertigo
may grip you after memories of whiffle-ball & fall air

turned aromatic. I looked him up & his tale took shape:
that littered overgrown North Bank's smokestacks

arcs of sulfur in the ozone, a bliss forever acid
& empty of suggestion. That filthy cathedral: a long-

abandoned shipyard where kids would go to smoke,
under its concrete pavilions, under graffiti & accidental

fountains a maze of rooms, feral splendor: a warren,
catacombs for what-you-will among left chemicals'

half-life seep. He wrote I humbly enclose a poem
of my own though regarding technique I know nothing

but would like to learn as who would not rather exist in
a bowl of painted fruit? You know that passion is unruly:

set ablaze by fragrance or a blood moon breaching Holland
Tunnel. In his poem there were radios & ermine, degrees

of translucence, troubles perceived as innumerable, wild
heifers, white sentiment & glitter & everything was really

the girl left in a rusted barrel hushed evermore in weeds
or coastal trash or catacombs & my spurious guilt

over the peculiar frisson in the details nevertheless will
not prevent me from telling you that the boys who finally

found her thought at first dog bones but then a sneaker.
Under each foundation there are many rooms, witnessed

by factory or dirty river, witnessed by the mistletoe
or whatever other bitter greens thrive even in the most

defiled soil. *And now you dimly remember leaving your best
purse on the subway. Money in it though the purse was a gift—*

And So Wax Was Made & Also Honey Out of the Tears of Re

When the wars are over & the checkpoints abandoned

when the cities wake as home to exotic birds who broadcast
      our coming & fertilize cracks in the asphalt, we'll stride

up the mountain like goatherds & make books from leaves
      of what trees spill most ambitious over the burned land.

When quarantines are lifted we'll play Marco Polo

in the empty wards & by lamplight study ancient methods
      of beekeeping: mud hive & yeast cake, the tendering

of tiny crowns & tiny homes of sedge. Practice the willing

exchange of smoke for song, box for circle, meat for bread
      & bread for radish—

yes, we will forgive even the generals, even the parliament
      of headless palms. When the wars are over

we'll offer oranges to tanagers & slick black seed to jays;
      when the curfews expire & all the debts default, though

there will always be dark rumors & dormant munitions

on no account may we cease waiting for the queen's
      emergence, so as long as there is something to barter

for this honey, for this wax that burns & leaves no ash.

Ouija Blink

Where to locate on that over-fingered lacquer speech?
  Over boundaries of corruption, the physics of corpse or ash?

The dead should lay back down. They make me itch. How
  to decipher in the arc of script a habited space

a hatch, hide, lookout, a porthole between yes & no
  between the moon & sun, a passage, peek or peep?

You know that it is only your hands the dead don't speak

(How the Dead Speak)

in the almost-heard tin ringing seconds past
  a motor's final shudder; the sickle's track on grass

or the chiffarobe that weeps clear sap, the tiny saint
  emerging from a pinto bean. In dreams where you must

quickly pack a satchel: all your books & glass, your inkwells
  ottomans & statuettes. You'll never make that plane.

The Association for the Prevention of Premature Burial
Thanks You

for your liberal contribution. It's pretty much what we expect
    from you fickle Victorians—

spawning Darwinists but leasing children, reading
    Byron in a poor light. You had certain fears:

Devolution, for example, à la Mr Hyde & live internment.

Nursery rhymes or prayers would liken death
    to sleep—*Sleep, pussy, die, shut your little eye*

—so truly was it that absurd? Given current theories
    about bad air & miasma, to fear revival

in a airless space, medals piercing your pre-tubercular chest?
    (*If I should die before*) Poe's true fear: entombed before

the spark has fled, the living taken with the dead: o you
    infamously syphilitic men awaiting suffocation,

souls lost 'mong heaps of bone, you soiled & poxed:
    wasn't it the grave robber most likely to espy

the patented device "permitting the awakened to pull
    a velvet cord which will activate a flag & bells" ?

Here I am, O resurrection man! A knock on the head
    & you're lifeless again: *Pussy eats dirt from a sky-blue plate*;

earth wins, a broken spade. Prophetic, you gentlemen:
a chapter between opium abuse & rampant prostitution.

from A Practical Guide to Hand Analysis *[tide]*

If the line of tragic fate runs to the base of your second finger
surely the assassin lifts a sputtered bee from punch
or puddle, cold coffee, what-have-you, so gently after
unrepented business in a hotel room or underpass
while the rest of us are so far spared inexplicably
from angry weather in the head, from black ice
or Impala, embolism, low clearance, cells amok—

Swaddled thus in luck we backslide. Rightly
you rebuke us, Cap'n, but should this lifeline split
or intrepid take a risky veer to thumb, I'll gladly
join you in the seam, arm & arm within whatever
star or calyx vacant, or some obliging tide-pool
adjacent a volcano where we'll reign as sea hares
in a warm & sentient froth, done with bones, withal.

In Central Asia Nomadic Horsemen
—A home without a morin khuur is like a widow

In Central Asia nomadic horsemen carved
horse-heads on the pegbox of their violins.

Early upright two-stringed, horsehair violins,
morin khuur: always carried on the saddle.

One hundred tail hairs for each stiff string,
taut spring on the sharp stroke. Thick whinny

& the black boughs' scrape in biting wind:
willows in a white light—glittered, frozen, bent

by bitter weather. The snap & slide of leather
strap on oiled saddle. Steel's exit from a sheath.

≈

Their burly horses chew dry grass & lick the snow—

Morin Khuur could make a song to calm the feral mare
or sooth the tame one's labor. To coax your foes'

remaining horses off of glory's gore-soaked field,
or to settle spirit chatter, the restless ancestors

of these surely superstitious early horsemen;
songs to stop their turnip skulls from stirring

under the endless steppe & winter's marshes
or under summer grass stretched tight with seed.

≈

The wood should be willow. The strings horse-tail.
The bow horse-tail. The face may be of newborn

lamb or camel skin. The resin larch or cedar. Legend
says that Sukhe made the first two-stringed violin

when his beloved horse was killed out of spite
by a jealous rival. Gut & muscle, coat & bone.

In a dream his horse came home to him
and said *now master make of me a two-stringed violin*—

Hatfield

Such lovely matter, rain, abundant rain,
though Sweetwater overflowed and Otay broke
I filled your reservoir as I was asked.

Yes twenty souls were lost, they say, or more;
still Hatfield was upbeat, knowing he'd arranged
the matter of such long-awaited rain. Come

from out of nowhere with a digging stick,
his secret chemicals & elemental price
to fill the reservoir as he was asked.

The rain was free, except his cost per inch.
Did San Diego never read a fairy tale?
Such weighty matter, that abundant rain—

On the Altiplano in a dry December, families
bake the dough-boy, dough-girl. Seeded children
ask the rain to fill the furrows, reservoirs.

Their teeth are pumpkin seeds, their eyes are beans.
Clothe them in paper, offer them fire.
I filled your reservoir as I was asked
with lovely matter: rain, the banquet rain—

In 1916, the "Rainmaker" Charles Malloy Hatfield was hired to fill the reservoirs near drought-stricken San Diego by his secret method of releasing chemicals into the air. It subsequently rained so heavily that the Otay and Lower Sweetwater dams broke. The number of deaths attributed to flooding is still a matter of dispute.

The House of Être

La Maison d'Être is a device for remembering which verbs use "etre" in the passé composé: tomber, venir, monter, etc.; intransitive verbs that take no direct object, as in

—Suddenly on a chill September morning, the trees turn

or

—Between the hall tree's brass tentacles & wild boar's head
        the loose tusks fall

& rolling loose make tracks on dusty tile. In Être's house
        some things are fake:
not the silver naturally or these placards urging revolution

but the bear-trap is a movie prop, that van der Aa
        a back-page ad.
The floors are slick. They said *Where have you been.* Tequila's

in the freezer. Come in. *Entre.* Rest here among inertia's
        static trove: geodes
& brass animals, defiled ivory, rest beneath this photo of

a locomotive rushing towards a frozen lake. If the train is
        always a story
of leaving & coming back, then come back to our brick

kitchen, our porch swing, our pantry of secret diminutives.
        Where have you been
again (again!); they said come back to paperweights ablaze

with light that conjures darting fish within them. Our
　　　imperfect hallway
shower provides what ablutions you require, witnessed

gratis by cheap perfumes' profusion. There are verbs
　　　you have to learn:
Get out. Come back. Don't fall down the shaft we never

see to *where* the daylight basement features unpaid cable,
　　　unrepentant
moths, the Ouija Board, music box & dirty books. *Have you*

descended narrow stairs where ivy comes through the cracks
　　　to scale the wall
& die? *Where?* In our house, my dear, our dark apartments—

from A Practical Guide to Hand Analysis *[ravine]*

if the line of the heart rising on the third finger
signals a love that is outwardly selfish and cold
we know the tightest figure-eight knot can be cut.
How much is instinct? The mare's insistence
on keeping between you & her foal; how in some
dreamed & luminous under-canopy the swiftlet
patiently makes her edible nest or the hornbill
seals herself in fever trees. How swallows
know what's up. Bird spit plus twigs: desired cipher,
a code once overheard & cracked at last. O waxing
palo verde, greasewood, elf owl, devil's claw.
O cactus wren. Ocatillo. I would be you, Ravine:
vigilant with insect din, shallow caves & webs.
Green thorns beset in darkness. Let no one in.

Report of The Chief Astronomer

—Upon the survey of the northwest angle of the Boundary Lake of the Woods to the summit of the Rocky Mountains, 1876.

(iii) Sir: Having the honor to transmit herewith
that to the hazards already named regarding
the isolation of these mauvias terres, I add
my men cold-gripped around the Sibley.
Their breath bog-steam through broke ice.

> *Sleepers awake! To beef sawed*
> *like limestone & a cup*
> *of snow. To vinegar chopped*
> *out of pots with a hatchet.*[1]

(vi) Sir: Having the honor to transmit herewith
the details of a fire: sometime after one o'clock
I beheld our tent in flames above my head.
All our efforts to extinguish it were futile:
we heaped the blaze with boughs instead.
I repaired a harness by the light bestowed.

> *At dawn the spirit thermometer,*
> *fixed to a tree, read*
> *at twenty-three below.*[2]

---

[1]   *from Cree a rough translation: February's ass—*
[2]   *And the pine pitch froze gold*

(xv) Sir: Having the honor to report
another clear night to get the azimuth

> *& that no more do I feel the cold—*
> *though for meat little grouse liver,*
> *hot in the paw—*

At intervals a wolf will humbly approach
& start with urgent moan the dogs

who begin gently, a soft collective sigh
then make their trembling crescendo.[3]

(xxi) As my tent floor was composed of ice
my souvenirs apart from one scorched harness
are two black toes.[4] The next day found us

high above the valley, in delightful weather:
a winter's Sunday stroll, complete with dogs!
Still at Midnight we were hours short the depot.[5]

> *Light broke the needles, but cold took the blame*

---

[3] *black thread in a skin quilt, gone—*
[4] *Jean passe moi ton conteau*
[5] *Gone, gone—*

(xxx) the stream whose position even my good scout Jean did not suspect
O Bedrock, brook ice, black hills astir:
I offer my frost face. Polaris, a posy of stars.
my lame foot & zenith, my vanishing trace.

It was romance bore me to this high divide:

the love between Milk River & Saskatchewan
& jealousy between the buttes

> *the slough arrayed in all her trampled sand*
> *the plum I palmed long shriven*[6]

---

[6] *under snow*

z

Sir Say Pray
Thomas Hardy

The milkmaids say *pray* for their speech is reserved,
    fixed here in circles of opalized light.

Presenting themselves without fancy or choice
    chapped hands on the full udder's verge,

y'know—cream-skinned, gathering toad-spume on skirts
    relentlessly cracking the snails underfoot—

A century later & more their compeers bow heads
    to the luminous fields made of ether,

of blue & extravagant air, calling up with the same
    nimble fingers their ciphered familiars,

girl-souls at large in a non-human hour.
    Speaking their argot & screen-practiced moue.

Not to *you*, with your paper, your man-heavy shoes,
    untouched by the mulch of the digital yard!

They only gaze rapt at threshold, milk spilled.
    No purchase for you here, Sir, & no clue—

our harvest is lattice and husk—

With a Court of Flies Attendant

It burns up all the grass too and breaks the stones, so tremendous is its noxious influence.
—Pliny the Elder: "The Serpents Called Basilisk," *Natural History*

On a blood- or honey-colored moon at midnight & no 60-watt abuzz. With
Sirius ascendant. From a dunghill's punk egg hatched

By toad or serpent. From cold gland & pillaged crib, from ruined sluice,
bible comics & potshots at swallows. From the Ring of Fire, the Zipper,

The Nighthawk with her victims taloned upside-down. From *pistis* to *gnosis*
To the midway where they draw a bead on cardboard sheikhs. From no harvest.

From no temperate father. From years borne down tainted water
& all we failed to mark in frequencies cranked up, from

How laughing we cast our own forfeit. O well—
It's cinch your boots up now, it's shoulder to the wheel, it's soldier on

To lay coins on the fang marks & stand already spent
Condemned for what we wrongly thought exhaustion.

Comes now the bright arrival, comes the pageant rain of ashes:
The seal torn & tablets fixed but still impossible to read.

Lithium Dreams (White Sea)

The Salar de Uyuni in Bolivia holds the world's largest lithium reserves.

—as remote & unlikely a place as can be imagined for the world to seek its salvation.

(Matthew Power)

Once, volcanoes walked & talked like humans. Married.
      Quarreled & gave birth. When the beautiful Tunupa's

husband ran away & took their only child she mourned:

she cried & stormed, her full breasts spilled until she made
      this sunken bed, a dry & ragged ice-white sea. Tears

& milk. Salt. Silver liquor of the spirits, the winter tuber's pulp.

≈

Buzz Aldrin spied a plain from space: twice Rhode Island-sized,

not a glacier but this vast evaporation, a place so flat we use its plane
to calibrate the altitude of satellites, measure the retreat of polar ice.

A dry lagoon of element. Energy. *Winking like a coin in a well.*

≈

In bare Salar the tourists bottle sand & salt: mug & pirouette
across this lithic sink of drought, empty leagues of sky & light,

slight mist of silt. We dream our dreams of clean—or *cleaner* —
means to drive and speak—o Li, atomic number three, be
our Miracle element!

Prehistoric smelt, simmered & distilled

in Aliplano climes, your samite matter known to quiet, after all,
the manic brain, the urge to suicide; proven to dispel the voice

that whispers *fire from the gods is never free*—
                                        Lithium chloride
& plain table salt under ancient ocean crust; fossils & algae;

A bird so bright & blackly drowned, pickled in the salt brine pool:
the desert is generous.
                        The desert is a pot boiled dry. This road

will turn to dirt and then to salt, to the workers in jumpsuits,
veiled & covered from the brutal sun; but we're not here, not *here*—

what matters are the distant cities: Chongching, Phoenix, Quebec,
Lagos, far & star-chalked: splitting at the seams. Now

                                ≈

the shrouded workers wait for sunset. The desert is patient.

They see the bed plowed under: slapdash trenches in the legend,

in the hasty furrows raked. With eyes narrowed from the endless
light. See *Litio*. Wages in the veins laid open; see paid the lush
reduction of her ditches' spill. This new abyss to feed our traffic.

Assume the Milk-White

bodies of agate. Draw close the bones of this biddable metal:
 chalice and ingot, gilt saints on cypress planks,

Agamemnon's mask unearthed. Sulfur & salt: the alchemist's
 scarred hands. Think men upon their knees

before the riverbed for that Black Hills silt, that sluice
 long girdled in the zigzag crack. O

that lucre. The worshipful company's murderous guilds—
 It's too late now to look away from that bright flame,

too late to take the value back from filigree
 or sacred blade, ransom-gilded Seric, idol,

from hidden trove or gently beaten fleece—South
 of Ulaanbaatar cranes decorate the skyline.

In the Congo children work the pit shifts. Mercury and silica
 will grace the margins of each living membrane's

tender stem & inch of lymph. All flesh thus tempered,
 thus fixed in the mine's dark mouth.

Ûdwr. Meaning *divine water.*
 Physika kai mystica: the secret things.

Our guide in Potosí lighting his cigar with dynamite:
 No se preocupe, trabajo por Sendero Luminoso! Hands

cupping the bright flame. Tracing the halo.
        The hoards turned up by English plowmen, amulets

in shafts along the overpass. Shields beaten thin
        and dropped unearthly to your brokerage screen, leverage

on the scale of equity. Percolated, according to Theophilus.
        from vinegar, red copper, human blood & ash of basilisk.[†]

†Consult page 25 for how to grow a basilisk

Dear Drought

Offer your usual posy of goat-heads. Proffer
sharp garlands of thistle & Incas' thin down;
of squash bugs strung on blighted stems; send

back necklaced every reeking pearl I crushed,

each egg cluster that I scraped away with knife
or twig or thumb-nail. Wake me sweat-laced
from a dream of hidden stables: the gentle foals

atremble, stem-legged, long-neglected. Dear
Drought our summer corn was overrun again
with weed & cheat; the bitter zinnias fell to bits.

Dear yearlings our harvest is lattice & husk.

Though from a distance it looked like a prison

that bastioned: our high school with its grim facade & archer slits
    for windows, what vivid mountains rose just west!

Notwithstanding lack of ventilation; classrooms stacked like cells
    around a courtyard webbed with refuse; despite R— C—

who killed his parents on that county road; despite the globes so
    dumbly pencil-scarred, our state a silver bruise; though

none can forget without effort catcalls (*fag*) in stairwells (*slut*); though I
    I was only an echo, a whirlwind, a little white heifer, a swan;

despite crepe-paper pageants; ditto homeroom, ditto stillborn pigs
    that we & suburbs' cruelest sons in eighty-six did grimly

flense, dissect & trim with pins; despite black-sharpied *Fuck* on brick;
    the queens & freaks, the jocks & born-agains & requisite

vaginas scribed in Chaucer's grimy crease; while bus fumes bloomed
    in skies alight with borealis & a burning shuttle; notwithstanding

the fields covered overnight in houses, the redolent lunchroom,
    the band spittoon's brass crash; despite (& now cue

a single soaring sour trombone's note!) all that I confess
    I thought to exorcise, when I bear my daughter to the same

steel doors I will say memory is a dark maze always—
    what else to do but call with hope or forged affection

on the softness of bleachers, the ether of ceilings;
  what else but paint in spirit green the reneged scene?

Flaubert & the Chancre

Despite Pigalle's most lightly-poxed & supple
minxes, I still considered it possible to be violent
in art but orderly in life: to stand at the cataract's
precipice in a pricy slicker, witness to the revolution,
island in the traffic, tiny shrine in dirty alleys;

to buy a ride, as it were, steadfast through the storm
until each hand-stitched banner finally wilts,
—until this hive's vile rise: reckoned as the will of god
or delinquent blood, at least: a weeping penalty:

love-sweats will shake you like a cheap sheet, *cher*—
your tongue thicken to an ox's, pronouncing words
that only through your industry still merit this translation:
I sometimes feel I am liquefying like an old Camembert

Among Us

The oily dishcloth in a tower of flame, sudden-
Like, the child briefly vanished: *I-thought-for-a-second—*

What fetches the adrenal swell, blush of nerves
Or taste of iron, the near smashup, sideswipe,

Blowout, a jack-knifed truck's adjacent trigger or
Jump in the mob's pulse, the certain & absurd

Stampede, the linchpin's twist & split at twenty
Thousand feet. The rutted pea-sized lump.

Your own house tossed, your door kicked in: this
Mess the only proof you need no matter's static

But will instead suffer uncomplainingly, even
Meekly, each derangement, all glanced static

I-thought-it-was, I thought it —when thought's not
Really in it. First your thalamus perceives

Some threat, then how the limbic ditch will run—
How pupils dilate in order to behold the old RV

Converted with swiped cobalt-60, flames drifting
Slo-mo into some annual do; to anticipate the quick

Abduction or all the fated plagues produced
In mobile labs that border semi-jungled slums

& tell us thus we need no corroboration to
Prove the hordes plot only god knows

What. Shed your reason, rouse the sleepers:
Comes now the cybertort, comes the rogue explosive

Robbed & lobbed, comes now the roaming ether's
Traffic & all those dark cells' secret chorus,

To the dread-mopped floor, the ambulance or cafe's
Abattoir and yes, you know *you know* it's coming.

My Family Versus Yours

What slapdash pact might fix this schism?

Manners are bequeathed by soil:
by clean sand yours claim hymnal sheets,

by peat mine the moonshine; still, can't we
fake accord between the over-parsing

of dead socialists & cobbling or grift?

A chapel basket & the holler's augur?
Where do tragic tenors figure in decayed tableaux?

Your family fawning over the dachshund

mine brawling, singing bawdy—
only we dippers can psalm such a trilling

and now all the daughters want to be cats.

Packs of grimalkin will always win, besides
my kith could fleece your kin & then some:

if vicars swan they still may whisper.

A French Piano Tuner & a One-Eyed Glassblower Walk into a Bar

Would you rather hear the louche pun drawn
    from *glory hole, lip wrap* or *fingering*

or hear a tiny hammer striking wire?
    Would you rather see the molten birthing glass?

Seat Eros next to Kronos, for the banter. I *heard*
    she's yet unplowed —I *heard your quiver dangled down*—

I heard you dwell in borrowed forms—*love's nothing*
    but glimmer-to-wither, dawn's fireflies expired.

In this place we sift & bounce the words like dice
    thrice dip a pipe into the magma, *o my stars.*

Lear & Gloucester walk into a bar
    debating again the color of bluffs or moors

or cormorants: *like craquelure like damp tea leaf*
    driftwood   no, peat steam   no, brined sand-apple ink

Were all your letters in fact suns?
    Forgotten, after all that trouble—

Are those bellows blowing some?
    A field of broken bottles, fragments blue.

A tune invented to divert a girl.

Three Meals
Aesop

In Vain A Swallow Seeks to Edify the Other Birds

demanding less chatter on the fence and much
more vigilance: the end comes quick (cat

pellet trap), so quick your snare of nerves
will never sense it: (owl or hawk). Never mind

the gnats. See that farmer sowing hemp & flax?
You must pick up every seed, must muster up

the appetite you'd find for scattered corn;
Swallow's anthem for the diligent: *Clean your plate*!

But the bushtits dart & flinch: enraptured, plumb
distracted by the cattails' rupture: sun & dust

made pixilate; the bitter waxwings only bicker
& hummingbirds are fighting over trumpet vine.

One day this crop will grow and come at last
to be pluck'd up & pill'd & dress'd & spun

then woven into nets & while others struggle
the swallow twitters *toldja* — as Warblers dwindle

toldja cocooning in the cord like spindles;
toldja while the Thrashers, stagy, faint & splay—

Minutes: The Frogs Meet to Chuse a King

On the one hand, order out of pestilence: out of broke-
yoke slime, this venue with no vista, tic in nature's

grandeur. Time that we consider how an Emperor
with regal silhouette might present us with an ordered

front, a States of Lakes; rank stagnancy to Empire;
no more backdoor bog but rules & visible horizon.

On the other, note one bile-geyser orchid, our
phosphorescent moss, the fly-trap's pressing

business of digestion & the greenheads driving
cattle to immersion. Note too our King's quick bill,

his feather belt. Next & next. Before the chambered
office, friends, his mortal pink & muscled gullet.

Aesop Serves a Meal of Tongues to his Master's Guests and
Predictably is Not Beaten

Waggish Aesop again forgiven by indulgent Xanthus
(ho-hum) even for serving to philosophers the organ
they called *Oracle of Wisdom.* Yes, a meal of only tongues:

tongues upon tongues, tongues upon toast, sliced
and furred with whitish buds like willow saplings
tongues in honey, glaze and ewe-fat syrup, roasted,

purpled underneath, just slightly charred on skewers.
Tongues fried, tongues basted, dressed or served in soup
taste & tasting, laid on plates; what clever slave would say

by serving tongues that tongues will do what they will do:
gossip, pleasure, bear false witness, ululate or scold
or wag, wag, wag. Long may your song outlast you.

"Prodigious fine land, but subject to wets and unhealthiness..."

We have been curiously entertained, of late, with the description of an engine lately constructed... for taking trees up at the roots.

—George Washington, Notes on the Dismal Swamp, 1783

What to make of mazes, cul-de-sacs in brackish landscape
bordering on sound? Your fortune, boy. We'll turn the brine,

burn the tongues of moss, ripe thorns, slack weep of sap—

until you're master of this phosphored froth & frogspawn,
this vine-blind bank & tangle, felons' thoroughfare, slaves'

otherwhere. We'll fill every acre, every back camp, every hollow

housed in redbud, scrub pine, cypress, gum & juniper. Realm
of ivory-bill & feral hog, secret orchids, secret corpses. Never

mind the constant din of carapaced, soil intricate but iron-poor.

Marshland makes the good farm by & by. Consider this black
steep bank at the foot of which begins your fertile valley fed

by Pharmick amber water: *so pure it's said to heal & mend, this*

estimable muck my Son upon which to build your causeway—

Ovid on the Poor Economy of Overgrazing
Io

Now she will feed on short & bitter grasses,
persistent weeds that come from overgrazing:

blue chicory, stink-cheat & ironweed. Thistle
will require several applications, so remove

meat animals a month before the slaughter.
Her water will be muddy, rude & over-stirred

her hoof-prints shallow pools for skimmers.
Black clusters wallow at the corners of my eyes

Her only couch, poor creature, will be ground:
willow shoots nub-gnawed & trampled pastures

so often very low in phosphorus and potash.
There, where I had fled to hide among the other heifers

She can only furrow dust with one forefoot
but the breeding season must not be delayed

so her mate will be selected from some herd,
her son a bullock. Nights, the hungry circle

in an unwatched field. Days, quick insects pester.
Speech is bawl & moo. *Am I just a branded slab*

Physician, Priest, Gravedigger

What was your profession in 1349?

Do you believe celestial retribution set this pest in motion?
Pick *sin* or *guild*. *Livid* or *lice*.
In a tight spot are you apt to speak up or keep wisely silent?
Pick *epoch* or *commerce*. Malthus or Marx.
For an evening out, do you prefer a foul ship's hold in Pisa port
a ditch in Askøy, or a brothel in Constantinople?
Now from this palate choose your favorite shade of black
but don't think too long!
Do you ever feel whittled by the pruner's knife
stripped gradually of every green string
every summer lush & blind, as though
your land's been tilled past bearing?
Pick *kin* or *kiln*. Pick abstinence or insurrection.
Alas, you were a corpse.

Ladies in the Ausgburg gardens, thieving pollen—

Confess

& you may yet be forgiven for any sinful behaviors, even ruination or cream-stealing. As He said

It seems we are now wandering into excursive speculations when our stated intention was merely to document

The day when tremors shook the square, the walls cracked & plaster crumbled. A sudden fire in the studio forced the evacuation of several costumed horses but the mayor's loyal guard were nowhere

inside the labyrinth of cafes for the wrongfully exiled, but who would give up their disguise willingly

when a nurse and orderly make bold to brush hands in the tubercular ward's narrow passage, exactly what is the price of that static? That frisson on much-abused skin, in this new order—especially in

light of the fact that assessors reported post-blast the skin of a Zeppelin, stereo cards of Pushmi-Pullyu & three violins with strings of resined hair. Some items had the stamp of a red hand on their

women will meet them ten or so abreast; even lamentations kept in cadence to the solemn chant by

God only knows your reasons for researching *sal volitile*, or for haunting the depot in such imprudent disregard for your reputation. Did you really take such errant pleasure in exaggeration. Tell me

Those who had a red stamp on their mouths: tell me, what does this signify if not the lifeblood of

whichever bankrupt kingdom holds your trifling allegiance? Confess. We
cannot force the gods to

The Madness of Crowds

Tulip

Long thought wrongly to be Turkish for *turban*

but as it was fashionable in the Ottoman Empire
to put tulips on turbans perhaps the translator

was confused having gone astray in alleys of Ordu

or Constantinople, where the flower had long been
popular. Ladies in the Augsburg gardens thieving

pollen, augment! Barges bright on the Zuyder Zee,

komen fill your holds with these immortal tubers:
each species well-recorded in these colored plates.

O Pompeius de Angelis! Lipsius of Ledyan! You
middle classes of Amsterdam and Hoorn: a silver

drinking cup, two grey horses & three tons of butter

for one rare bulb of *Semper Augustus*, the very same
a luckless Haarlem sailor once plucked as lunch

thinking it an onion, some relish for his herring—

Witch

The record quotes one Margaret Arnold. Your Honor:
Myself I saw the children swallow bees, then vomit
crook'd pins, two-penny nails, splinters & a vile froth

On her pillow we found cakes of feathers large
as crown pieces, placed in a curious order.

                      (Making *radii*, your Honor—)

a star-shaped onion, some bewitched pigs, a mouse
that thrown into the fire shrieked like any whelp

                         (the maid-servant—was she deposed?)

Their wives having transformed themselves to cats were burned forthwith.

They kept a careful record of the names.

Song

Cherry Ripe! Cherry Ripe! Ripe I cry,
Full and fair ones
Come and buy

London Hospital 187-

My Dearest Zee,

I keep a record of their faddish phrases: *Cherry Ripe*
was a plague lasting near nine-month. Young men & old,

wives & widows, maid servants were all alike musical
fishermen, loose women, all the idle in town—

My dear, the popular humors of this great city
are a constant source of amusement to me
whose sympathies are amenable enough
to embrace this madness though I be refined.
The ice bathes having failed, they try a sugar cure

                    (The vox populi had wore itself hoarse.)

Relic

In Paris is kept with great care a thorn
nail-clippings mulberry Christ's tears

& on the street they'll sell you hanks of hair
  toe bones encased in their own small coffins.

Come and buy!
               (happy is the sinner)

In Naples shreds of garment from the luckless
Masaniello, a fisherman raised high by mob favor
then shot like a mad dog, spat on & quartered

by & by he was unburied & arrayed in royal robes

his torso, at least, and the village women
later tore his wooden door off its hinges

                                        (who possesses)
for splinters—

                              (Z, the fisherman—was he?)

Nonce for the Gizzard

For now discount the braggart plumage
and pity instead her onerous chore:

this factory that has no task except
to nurse the husk or grind it, gastric urn

for the crop's excess, chock-a-block
& still she'll mince it: right down

to her last inch of muscle & flint.
Would you be an altar or a engine?

A knickknack or a neat teaspoon? Better
anyway to be no general guts

but this mill in the innards, always busy
while they marvel at the wattle

& the sprightly mite-infested feathers;
busy grotto for the kernel

for every little pip picked up, every pebble
shoveled down the gullet by a greedy beak

Isle of the Narrator

It's true these boots were taken from a dead man,
but he'd already drown'd: I didn't want his purse.

It's true I've carried infant bones within a kettle
but for the purposes of study only, brother

trust me: you & I are royal twins, operatically estranged—
observe our matching birthmarks, side & thigh! Sister,

come ashore: nights here are Dionysian: crowns
of thicket, silly incense & umbilic torches,

horns & holy rattles attend the garlanded bull.
Though convictions and my eyeteeth dim in daylight

our severance is too high a price to pay for truth.
And anyway you didn't voyage here for truth

from A Practical Guide to Hand Analysis *[urchin]*

if crosses which appear here & there in the hand
tell of keen observation but also delusions—
Well, sure. Observing after all is not the same
as *knowing*; words that were clear yesterday
may appear today as Hittite, the way your
own street looks different in the rain or how
underwater you can never tell volcano limpets
from dwarf keyholes. Problems begin when
after reasonable effort, you cannot identify
a specimen. Which shell is spoon-shaped, which
which is dish? Ivory, pearl, or ash? Then comes
the check for gills & hinges, come the urchin
spines, or worse, their beaten seep: armless
now & eyeless. Blind. Bankrupt by the rudder.

For Fresno's Best Process Service Call Hermes

True, my office is a gold Camino nineteen eighty-two
    & front-work's on a laptop, but there are older tricks:

this knack I have to spy a sham address: figures
    pried off siding or the silhouette that's left

when eight is changed to three; my talent to discern
    the perp who hides behind the car or ducks among

the bins or sidles, slams the screen & tries
    for silence then behind his gutted door. Some

will wave a gun or summon dogs. Once a rooster.
    Once an Alderman who menaced with a mallet

(croquet) when his trucking company was sued
    & there's still this lucent bruise on my right heel—

long story: swan-shot, tree house, veteran. Though
    no one wants this dachshund's weight of paper

compiled by some paralegal underpaid in Phoenix,
    I assure you I will always serve. I am the envoy

(a ball caps hides my third eye). Put me in swift shoes
    or wings, at some cosmic door with only sky behind—

black-clad, Prophet of Xerox, steadfast
    bearer of a Clerk Court's smeared truncated seal.

I know these streets: the houses boarded up,
  the other heralds driving slow on fractured blacktop;

the sidewalks' glass & fenders scattered; vacant quarter
  acres returning now to palm & pampas, trees of heaven.

I am waiting at the crossroads, here at your broken gate
  where barbed acacias stoop to shade my trespass.

Whole Cities Burn for Your Account Number
Phaethon

Your urgent assistance needed with absolute trust.
I swear I never touched those horses of my father
nevertheless without trial I was accused of plots

when Caucasus burned & Ossa burned, and Pindus—
So I must solicit your strictest confidence in this
matter. I think you can be of Greatest Help to me!

I am PHAETHON, son of the god HELIOS

who deposited for me the sum of $17.5 million
before Xanthus knew a second burning, though
I beg you would keep that information private

as well as leaves burnt crisp & crops made tinder
(because of my country's unending political crises)
& that my sisters turned to poplars in their grief.

Madame, I respectfully offer you 12 percent despite

the unsteered chariot spokes & wheels thus shattered.
What grace I did escape with God's help & UN soldiers
(my hair still smoking with the fire of that forked bolt)

to Amsterdam where security companies are reliable
though all other peopled kingdoms into ashes turn.
Please confirm receipt & quote the reference number,

all burning, burning, and the wreckage scattered far.

After The Last Return—

tax, that is—relinquished with the official certificates
citing cause of death as chronic sentimentality,
I carried out his final demands, burning dance cards
& selling the gold claim cheap to an old poker rival.
But since I so far lack resolve to jettison love letters
penned from the Holocene or Dismal's fringe, deeds
to the cantaloupe fields, bills past due for my birth
cached with coupons for cremation; I appeal to you,
my dissolute kin who came to the funeral & left
before dawn the next day. Spring rain was promised us
but we know this house will vanish thus in dust & soon—
so what to do with heirloom spoons & milagritos,
monograms on mildewed linen, all the unsent checks?

Leviathan

Can you coax him from his house after the worst fall
  and keep him for weeks in a rehab?
²Can you put him in a nursing home they now call
  something else?
³Will he sign those papers with a shaky hand but
  nevertheless joke with the admissions director
    so that she says he's *spunky*?
⁴So that she says *o he's a character* and *there's life in him yet*—
⁵Will he demand to visit his house? And rage about mail you threw away?
⁶Will he rattle his walker? Will he shout about the lost receipts
  and catalogues, the free address labels, appeals from the GOP?
    Bright nickels taped to paper?
⁷If you lay a hand on his mail, you will remember the battle;
  you will not do it again.
⁸Any hope of subduing him is false. Who can make him wear hearing aids?
⁹Who can make him stick to his diet? Who can keep him from driving?
¹⁰I will not keep silence concerning his distended belly,
  all his limbs grown spindly,
    his terrible feet.
¹¹Who can keep him from drinking? His breath sets coals ablaze;
  phlegm erupts from his throat. *His undersides are jagged potshards.*
¹²Against him neither poison ivy nor oak nor AARP could avail.
¹³With what road in our vast & savaged west, with what town, what find,
  what basin was he not acquainted?
¹⁴What old deal did he not know the use of?
¹⁵Behind him he leaves a shimmering wake of iron
  bronze, spirits, tin, brushstrokes, water-pics & q-tips
    expired medications, Hawaiian shirts, ammunition
      silver, earth, paper, ashes—

¹⁶What stone could you bring him that he did not know the name of?
¹⁷Nothing on earth was his equal.

NOTES

Assume the Milk White
 "Let them assume the milk white bodies of agate/Let them draw together the bones of the metal" is from Ezra Pound's "The Alchemist"

Report of The Chief Astronomer
 is based on *Upon the Survey of the Boundary from the Lake of the Woods to the Summit of the Rocky Mountains 1876* by Captain W. J. Twining

Amy Beeder is the author of *Burn the Field and Now Make An Altar* (Carnegie Mellon University Press). A recipient of an NEA Fellowship, a "Discovery"/The Nation Award and a James Merrill Fellowship, she has worked as a creative writing instructor, freelance writer, reporter, political asylum specialist, sous-chef, high-school teacher in West Africa, and an election and human rights observer in Haiti and Suriname. Her work has appeared in *Poetry, The Kenyon Review, Ploughshares, AGNI, The Southern Review* and many other journals. She lives in Albuquerque.

RECENT AND SELECTED TITLES FROM TUPELO PRESS

Shahr-e-jaanaan: The City of The Beloved (poems)
by Adeeba Shahid Talukder

The Nail in the Tree: Essays on Art, Violence, and Childhood (essays/visual studies)
by Carol Ann Davis

Exclusions (poems)
by Noah Falck

Arrows (poems)
by Dan Beachy-Quick

Lucky Fish (poems)
by Aimee Nezhukumatathil

Butterfly Sleep (drama)
by Kim Kyung Ju, translated by Jake Levine

Canto General: Song of the Americas (poems)
by Pablo Neruda, translated by Mariela Griffor with Jeffrey Levine,
Nancy Naomi Carlson, and Rebecca Sieferle

Franciscan Notes (poems/memoir)
by Alan Williamson

boysgirls (hybrid fiction)
by Katie Farris

Diurne (poems)
by Kristin George Bagdanov

America that island off the coast of France (poems)
by Jesse Lee Kercheval

Epistle, Osprey (poems)
by Geri Doran

Hazel (fiction)
by David Huddle

See our complete list at tupelopress.org

Printed in the USA
CPSIA information can be obtained
at www.ICGtesting.com
LVHW090209240324
775348LV00002B/3